First published 1977
Macdonald Educational
Holywell House
Worship Street
London EC2

© Macdonald Educational
Limited, 1977

ISBN 0 382 06124 1

Published in the
United States by
Silver Burdett
Company, Morristown, N. J.

Library of Congress
Catalog Card No. 77-86183

Editor
Philippa Stewart

Assistant Editor
Caroline Russum

Design
Robert Wheeler

Production
Rosemary Bishop

Illustrators
Cathy Barton/B. L. Kearley
Peter Connolly
Hayward Art Group
Tony Payne
Mike Whittlesea/Temple Art
Eva Wilson

Consultant
Anne Ross MA PhD
(Celtic Studies and
    Archaeology)
University of Southampton

Photographs
Aerofilms Ltd: 19
Alinari: 47
Ashmolean Museum: 29
Janet Bord: 53
British Museum: 11
Department of Archaeology,
    University of Newcastle: 35
Werner Forman Archive (National
    Museum, Copenhagen): 42

Fürböch/Landesmuseum Johanneum,
    Graz, Austria: 10
Institut Belge: 50
Professor Megaw, University of Leicester: 41
Musée des Antiquités Nationales,
    St Germain-en-Laye, France: 26
National Museum, Copenhagen: 32
Ronald Sheridan: 52
Staatliche Museen zu Berlin: 55

The Celts

Robin Place

Macdonald Educational

The Celts

The Celts were one of the great peoples of Europe in the 500 years before Christ. From a homeland north of the Alps, they spread east and west, from Anatolia (in modern Turkey) to Spain and Britain. Raiding bands fought their way into Italy and Greece, looking for plunder and new lands in which to settle.

The Celts were a people full of contradictions. They spent much of their time fighting, often among themselves. Their religion involved sacrifice to the gods, with animal and even human victims. But they were not an uncivilized people: they included many fine craftsmen who produced objects of great beauty and artistic skill.

The Celts never united, and did not establish a great empire. They were divided into many tribes, who were continually squabbling. This intertribal rivalry was the cause of the Celts' eventual defeat by the Romans. One by one the Celtic tribes were brought within the Roman Empire, except for those in the far north of Scotland and in Ireland. There the old way of life went on into Christian times.

Much of the history of the Celts has been preserved in the writings of Greek and Roman travellers and historians. Information about the Celtic way of life can also be found in stories told to the early Christian monks in Ireland. We also know a great deal about Celtic life in pre-Roman times from the excavations of archaeologists, who have dug up the remains of many ancient farms, hillforts and sanctuaries all over the Celtic world.

All these sources of information have been used in this book, to give a picture of this brave and colourful people as they were before they were subdued by the Romans.

Contents

Barbarians across the Alps

▲ Greek traders from Massilia (Marseilles) have arrived at the hillfort of a Celtic chief. They find its little thatched houses very primitive compared with the stone buildings of their own cities. As the Celts do not speak Greek, they have brought along an interpreter to help with the hard bargaining.

Greek travellers in about 500 BC were the first people to write about the tribes of barbarians living across the Alps in central Europe. They called them "Keltoi", the Greek form of our word "Celts". At this time the Greeks were the most civilized people in Europe. Greek cities lived by trade and founded colonies on the shores of the Mediterranean Sea. Massilia, the modern Marseilles in France, was founded in about 600 BC. From there Greek traders followed the River Rhône into the heart of central Europe, where the Danube rises. Here they met and traded with Celtic tribes. The Celts were tall and fair and they appeared very strange to the short, olive-skinned Greeks.

To the Greek traders the Celts seemed a barbaric and very uncivilized people. They had no cities with fine buildings, they could not speak Greek and they did not write. But they were valuable customers. The Celtic chiefs were very fond of wine, which was brought from Greece by ship, in thick pottery jars called "amphorae". They also wanted wine-cups, and bronze flagons to pour the wine from. These imports were greatly prized and many have been found in the graves of Celtic chiefs.

In exchange, the Celts probably gave the Greeks salt, which was useful for preserving food, war prisoners to be used as slaves, some copper and tin, and perhaps cloth, hunting dogs and salted food.

▲ The Celtic chief is about to test the cup of wine that has been poured for him from the large "amphora". On the right a Greek trader is displaying pots and wine-cups painted with scenes of Greek life. In the background are slaves who will be offered to the Greeks in exchange for their goods.

17791

9

Who were the Celts?

The Celts occupied central and western Europe before the time of Christ. Forms of their language are still spoken. From it developed Irish and Scottish Gaelic, Welsh, Breton and other languages spoken in recent times by descendants of the Celts.

To find the ancestors of the ancient Celts, we have to rely on the evidence of archaeology. The people called Celts by Greek and Roman writers left pottery, tools and weapons buried in the ground. Archaeologists have called this period the "La Tène culture" after a site in Switzerland. This culture began about 500 BC, and is distinguished by fine pottery and decorated metalwork.

La Tène objects are very similar to those of an older culture called "Hallstatt", which began about 700 BC in Austria, so the Hallstatt people must have been Celts too. They lived in hillforts and their craftsmen were the first ones north of the Alps to use iron.

Archaeologists can also see links between Hallstatt objects and those of the older "Urnfield culture" that began in central Europe about 1200 BC, and may also have been Celtic. These warlike farmers cremated their dead, and buried the ashes in urns in great cemeteries, or "urnfields".

▲ This bronze sword-hilt in the shape of a man was made by a La Tène smith.

▼ A strange group of bronze figures on wheels, made by a Hallstatt smith. In the centre is a goddess. Around her are mounted warriors and sacred animals. The cult car was used in ritual. It was found at Strettweg in Austria and is 35 cm long.

The spread of Celtic culture

The Urnfield culture developed about 1200 BC in south Germany, Switzerland and Czechoslovakia. About 700 BC the Hallstatt culture developed in Austria and south Germany, spreading into France, Spain and Britain. The La Tène culture started around the River Rhine about 500 BC and spread east to Hungary and Switzerland, and west to France, Britain and Spain.

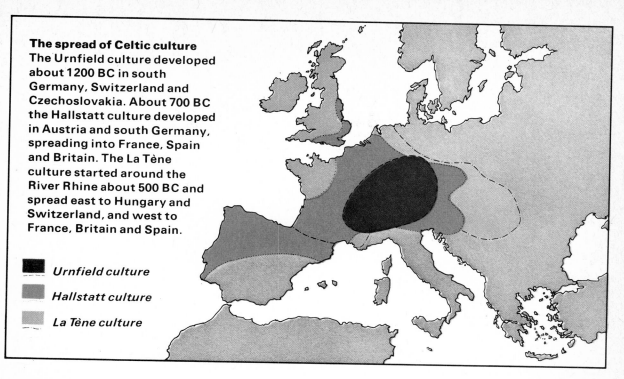

- ■ *Urnfield culture*
- ■ *Hallstatt culture*
- ■ *La Tène culture*

Celtic art

Celtic art was based on abstract, often geometric patterns, and frequently showed sacred animals and birds. The pottery plate below, made by a Hallstatt craftsman, has geometric patterns cut into its surface.

The later La Tène culture carried on many of the Celtic traditions, but also borrowed from Greek, Etruscan and Persian art. In shape and decoration this bronze wine flagon (right) is like many Greek examples; but the sacred duck on the spout is unmistakably Celtic. The flagon is one of a pair found in a La Tène grave in Lorraine, France.

The Champion's Portion

Roman and Greek writers described the Celts as boastful and noisy, and very fond of quarrelling. This was most obvious during their feasts.

Feasts were an important part of a Celtic noble's life. Often the feasting was to celebrate a victory in battle. Warriors would be given the chance to boast about their exploits. Before the meat was carved, there was a boasting contest to decide who was the greatest warrior present. Challengers for the title were egged on by their supporters to ever more extravagant claims. The winner was awarded the honour of carving the joint, and of taking the upper hind leg, or "Champion's Portion", for himself.

When different tribes were feasting together it was a matter of honour for the whole tribe for one of their men to be awarded the Champion's Portion. No-one seemed to care about the meat getting cold while the contest continued. Sometimes the meal ended before it had begun, in a fight, with casualties on both sides.

Accounts of contests for the Champion's Portion are given in two famous stories told among the Celts in Ireland for hundreds of years. They were later written down by Christian monks. These stories are "Bricriu's Feast" and "The Story of Mac Datho's Pig". Part of one of the stories is given below.

Extract from the Story of Mac Datho's Pig, which was written down in the 9th or 10th century AD.

Each of them brought up his exploits in the face of the other, till at last it came to one man who beat everyone —Cet mac Matach. He took his knife in his hand, and sat down by the pig.

"It shall not be," said a tall fair warrior, stepping forth, "that Cet carve the pig."

"Who is this?" said Cet.

"Angus, son of Lam-Gabaid (Hand-Wail), a better warrior than thou."

"Why is his father called Hand-Wail?" said Cet.

"We do not know, indeed," said all.

"But I know," said Cet. "Once I went eastward. An alarm was raised against me, and Hand-Wail came up with me. He made a cast at me. I cast back the same spear at him, which struck off his hand. What brings the son of that man to stand up to me?" said Cet.

So Angus sat down defeated.

What the Celts looked like

The Celts were tall, fair and well-built. The Romans who fought them in battle remarked on their terrifying appearance, particularly their hair. Celtic warriors soaked their hair in water mixed with crushed chalk to make it thick and pale in colour. Then they scraped it back towards the nape of the neck, and it dried very stiff, like a horse's mane. In later Irish tales there are descriptions of warriors whose hair was so stiff that an apple could be speared on the ends!

The Celts were not all fair, but dark-haired men seem to have bleached their hair, possibly with stale urine and ashes. Cu Chulainn, the hero of many Celtic tales, appears in one story with hair of three colours: dark at the roots, red in the middle, and golden yellow at the ends. The description suggests that the dye he had used was growing out.

Although some wore beards, most Celtic men had moustaches only. These were long and straggly. One Roman writer said: "the nobles let their moustaches grow so long that their mouths get covered up; and so, when they eat, these get entangled in the food, while their drink is taken in, as it were, through a strainer".

Celtic women were also tall and well-built. They had long hair which they wore either flowing or braided, and they decorated it with gold and bronze ornaments. They took a pride in their appearance and would dye their brows black and darken their lips and cheeks with elderberry juice.

▲ A bronze brooch used to fasten a tunic or cloak. It is rather like a safety pin, and was the invention of the Urnfield ancestors of the Celts.

▲ This massive bronze armlet is one of a pair found in Scotland. It was originally inlaid with red enamel. Both men and women wore armlets of gold and bronze.

▲ From the late 1st century BC, Celtic women in Britain used fine bronze mirrors. One side was polished so that they could see in it. The back was decorated with an ornate pattern shaded with criss-cross lines like basketwork. The elaborate handle was cast in bronze.

▲ Celtic women often wore necklaces of coloured glass beads. These were strung on cord which was made from plant fibres.

A Celtic warrior and his family. The Celts wore brightly coloured clothes, often of checked or plaid wool. Men wore trousers called bracae, and women a long tunic. Over these they used long cloaks fastened with a brooch, and many gold and silver ornaments. Poorer people wore simpler, less gaudy clothes, often with no jewellery.

15

The tribe

Servants

Farmers

Craftsmen

Warriors

King or Queen

Druids

◀ The structure of Celtic society. At the head of the tribe was a king or queen, chosen from among the descendants of a common great-grandfather. The chief was supported by his warriors, who received valuable gifts in return for fighting for him. The druids, as priests and lawgivers, were in many ways more important even than the chief.

Craftsmen held a particularly high position. The farmers, though lower in status, were free men not slaves. There were servants, who included women captured in war, but there was no slave class as in Greece or Rome.

▼ When he came of age, a nobleman's son would receive arms. Until this time he was brought up in the household of another noble, and was returned to his family only when his training as a warrior was complete. Girls too were fostered until they were old enough to be married.

Unlike the Romans, the Celts never united as a single nation. They were divided into many tribes, each ruled by its own chief, either a king or a queen. Sometimes the chief of a small tribe would give hostages to the chief of a stronger tribe, who in return would come to his aid if he were attacked. But there was too much rivalry between tribes for them to remain allies for long. Even when under attack from the Romans, the Celts of France and Britain did not unite. Some tribes fought on the Roman side against their fellow-Celts because of old quarrels.

Within the tribe there were several kins, or large families. The kin was responsible for keeping its members in order. If someone committed a crime against another member of the tribe, he was fined. The fine varied according to the victim's position in society, and was given to the family of the victim as compensation. An "honour-price" was fixed for all crimes, even murder. This was originally paid in cows. All members of a man's kin had to contribute to pay the fine. This made the kin want to restrain its more unruly members.

Celtic laws were never written down, but were passed on from generation to generation by word of mouth. The druids, who were the priests and lawgivers, learnt the laws by heart, probably in the form of poetry. There were no policemen to make sure the laws were kept. Caesar wrote that the greatest punishment for a Celt was to be forbidden to take part in tribal sacrifices.

Hill-top towns

Hillforts were the centres of Celtic tribal life. These defended settlements built on the tops of hills were the first towns north of the Alps. Traces of them can be seen today in many parts of Europe, from Spain to Roumania and from southern France to the Baltic. There are, for example, about 3,000 hillforts in Great Britain alone.

Building a hillfort was very hard work. Where stone could be found locally, huge loads were brought to build the ramparts, which could be up to 10 metres thick. In many hillforts, the ramparts were built round a framework of wooden posts. To make the framework, trees were cut down and the branches trimmed. The heavy trunks were then carried up the hill and set in deep post-holes, dug with iron or deer-antler picks.

▼ Women collecting water from the local well. This was an important part of their daily routine. Cattle were probably driven down to the nearest river or stream to drink.

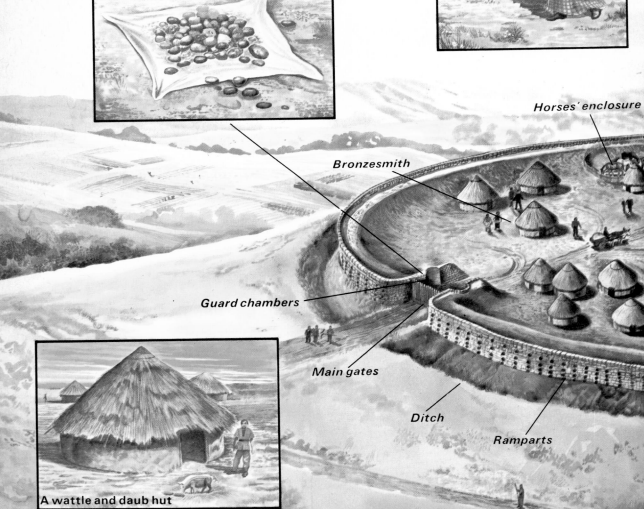

A pile of slingstones

Horses' enclosure

Bronzesmith

Guard chambers

Main gates

Ditch

Ramparts

A wattle and daub hut

In some cases the hillfort was the tribal capital. It guarded its territory, which was usually bounded by natural features such as rivers and swamps. Hillforts were defended with one, two or three ramparts. The easiest part to attack was the entrance, and this was closed with wooden gates. Inside the gates were piles of slingstones, ready to be hurled as attackers approached.

The houses of the chief and of his warriors and their families were built inside the hillfort. Many servants lived there too, to prepare the food and look after the weapons. Craftsmen also lived in the hillfort, making weapons and chariots. Only the farmers lived outside the walls, but they came into the hillfort for protection in times of war.

Celtic houses were built either of stone or, more usually, of wattle and daub with a wooden framework, and were thatched with straw. The chief's home was the largest. Dotted around the dwellings were pits where grain was stored. After a few years' use they were filled with rubbish.

▲ Maiden Castle in Dorset is a fine example of a Celtic hillfort. It covers 45 acres, and was defended by three ramparts and ditches. The ditches were 6 metres deep and 15 metres wide. Despite its elaborate defences, the Romans captured it in the 1st century AD.

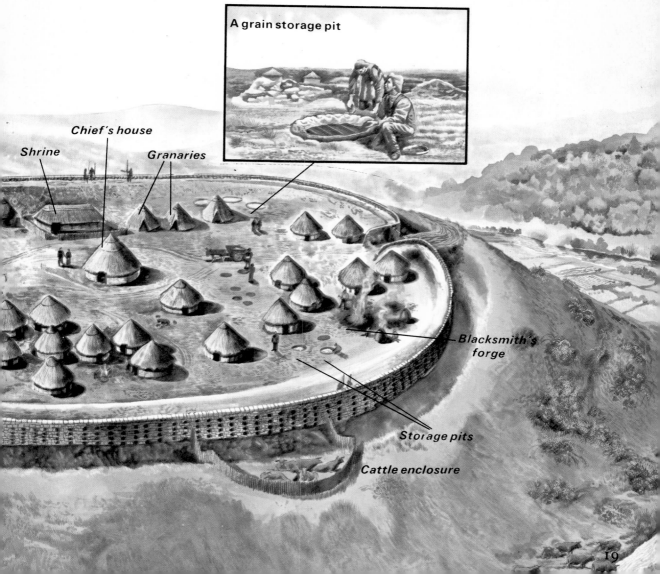

A grain storage pit

Shrine

Chief's house

Granaries

Blacksmith's forge

Storage pits

Cattle enclosure

A tribe of Celts storming the gates of a hillfort. The defenders are hurling slingstones and spears to try to stop the invaders from scaling the ladders and entering the settlement. The noise would have been tremendous. A Roman writer wrote of the "dreadful din" as the sound of the horns and trumpets mixed with the deafening war-cries of the warriors.

Attack on the gates

Celtic hillforts were often under attack from neighbouring tribes. The defences were therefore very important. Hillforts were protected by high ramparts and deep ditches, which made it difficult for an enemy to storm them. The Romans captured hillforts by besieging them and waiting for the Celts to surrender for lack of water. But among themselves the Celts did not wage war by siege. They were too warlike and impatient to wait for days until the defenders gave themselves up. Instead they would storm the hillfort's wooden gates, which were its weakest point.

To protect the gates, ramparts were turned either outwards or inwards to form a long passage, along which attackers had to fight every inch of the way. The defenders stood on the top of the ramparts, protected by a palisade, and hurled slingstones and spears, sometimes from specially built towers. Traces of elaborate entrances can still be seen at many sites. Skeletons of young men with savage cuts on their bones have been found at the entrances of some hillforts, showing that fierce fighting had taken place at the gates.

Hillforts and their defences were carefully planned; the Celts were good military engineers. Huge gangs of workers had to be directed in digging the ditches and tipping their loads of soil exactly where the rampart was to rise. The ramparts followed the contours of the hill and were carefully sited so that they gave a clear view in all directions, making it impossible for an enemy to approach without being seen.

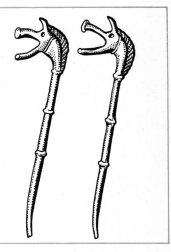

The Celtic war trumpet or "carnyx". Men blowing the carnyx are shown on the Gundestrup cauldron (see page 32). The sound came out of an animal's head made of bronze and mounted at the end of a long, vertical tube. A bronze boar's head, part of a carnyx, has been found at Deskford in Banffshire, Scotland. It dates back to the 1st century AD.

Digging up a hillfort

Archaeologists have dug up hillforts to discover how the defences were built and how the inhabitants lived. In most soils human and animal bones survive a long time and so provide evidence for meals and burials, but materials such as wood and cloth rot away. The only traces left by wooden posts, for example, are round, dark stains in the ground, marking the ancient post-holes.

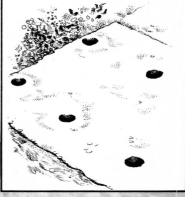

The ramparts
Archaeologists have dug trenches through the ramparts of hillforts and found traces of the post-holes shown above. From these they can tell how the walls were constructed. Pairs of big posts were set up about 2½ metres apart and linked by cross-timbers. These "boxes" were then filled with rubble.

Animal sacrifice
Archaeologists have found evidence for animal sacrifices at various Celtic sites. Whole skeletons of sheep, pigs and cows, as on the right, have been found buried in separate pits. If the animals had been killed for eating, the bones would have been scattered. The sacrifices were conducted by druids, who chanted prayers as the animal, with its throat cut, was lowered into the pit. The sacrifices were intended to please the gods.

Foundation burial

The body of a young man is being offered to the gods in a solemn ceremony by the druids. Human skeletons like the one above have been found in pits under the ramparts at some hillforts. Archaeologists believe that human sacrifices were made to the gods while the foundations of the ramparts were being built. In return the tribe hoped that the walls would have the protection of the gods.

A shrine

Archaeologists excavating the hillfort at South Cadbury in Somerset found traces of the trenches and post-holes shown above. They were not like any other building and there were no remains from meals or broken pots on the floor to show that people had lived there. The archaeologists decided it was probably a shrine for the worship of the gods. The shrine was sacred ground where only the druids could enter. Since geese were sacred, they would have wandered freely around the shrine.

A Celtic home

A Celtic home was a hive of industry. The Celts made their own food and clothes. Most women spent their time cooking and preserving food, spinning and weaving cloth, and bringing up children. Children and old people helped with the household tasks. The housewife in the picture is boiling meat for the family in a big metal cauldron.

A fine wooden bucket with decorated bronze bands. It was found in a grave.

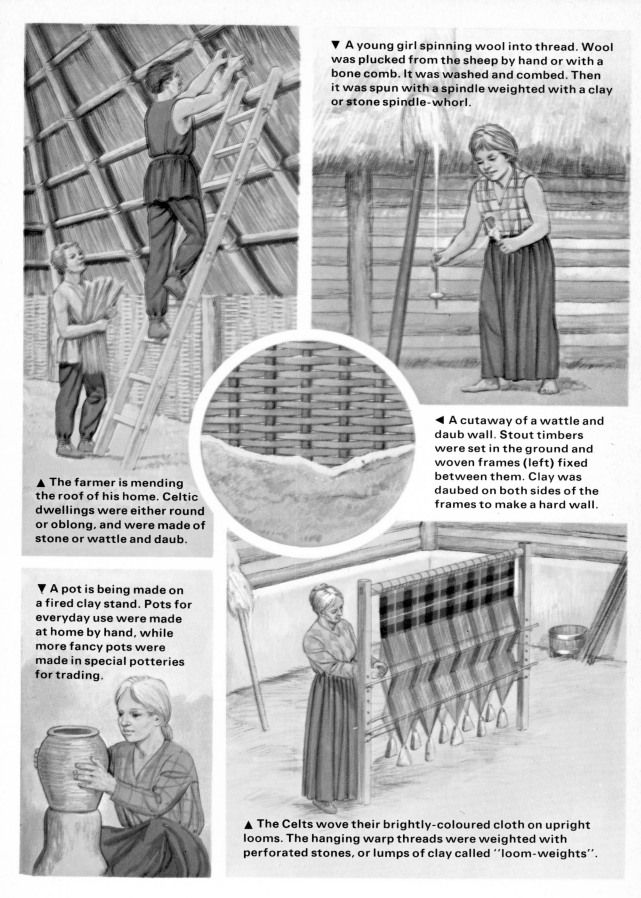

▼ A young girl spinning wool into thread. Wool was plucked from the sheep by hand or with a bone comb. It was washed and combed. Then it was spun with a spindle weighted with a clay or stone spindle-whorl.

◄ A cutaway of a wattle and daub wall. Stout timbers were set in the ground and woven frames (left) fixed between them. Clay was daubed on both sides of the frames to make a hard wall.

▲ The farmer is mending the roof of his home. Celtic dwellings were either round or oblong, and were made of stone or wattle and daub.

▼ A pot is being made on a fired clay stand. Pots for everyday use were made at home by hand, while more fancy pots were made in special potteries for trading.

▲ The Celts wove their brightly-coloured cloth on upright looms. The hanging warp threads were weighted with perforated stones, or lumps of clay called "loom-weights".

Food and drink

◄ A Celtic nobleman brandishing a spear as he rides off with his dog in pursuit of a wild boar. This bronze hunting scene on wheels comes from Merida in Spain and may have been used in ritual.

The Celts enjoyed their food and drink. They ate a great deal of meat. Domestic animals were kept to provide them with beef, lamb and pork. But the men also hunted game such as wild boar and deer. Fish were caught in rivers, and the women and children of tribes living near the sea collected shellfish. They may also have boiled edible seaweed with milk to make the nourishing white "carrigeen" still eaten in parts of Ireland today. Wild fruits, nuts and herbs were also picked. Herbs were used not only in cooking tasty dishes, but also, if picked at the right phase of the moon, to make medicines.

With their meat the Celts ate bread. Each family baked its own bread, from corn grown by the farmers. Porridge was also eaten, either with salt or else sweetened with honey. Milk was used to make cheese, which was strained in pots with holes drilled through the base.

The Celts mined salt, and they also made it by evaporating seawater. It was very valuable not only for seasoning food, but for preserving meat. Dried or salted meat was popular and could be kept for long periods to be eaten when food was scarce.

▼ This fine wooden tankard, decorated with bronze, held about 2 litres of wine! Celtic warriors probably passed around vessels like these at their feasts. One Roman author wrote: "They use a common cup, drinking a little at a time, not more than a mouthful, but they do it rather frequently"!

▲ A pottery jar for storing food.

▼ Breadmaking in the home. The woman on the left is grinding corn in a quern (handmill) to make flour. The young girl is fetching water which will be mixed with the flour into dough. The dough is then shaped into loaves and put in the domed clay oven to cook.

Meat was roasted on spits, or boiled in pits in the ground. The pit was filled with water. Then stones made hot in a bonfire were lifted with green sticks and dropped into the water. 450 litres of water could be brought to the boil in this way in half an hour. Joints were also boiled indoors, in metal cauldrons hung over the fire on strong chains, which were fixed to the rafters of the roof.

Drink was an important part of Celtic meals. Chiefs imported wine from Greece and Italy, but every family made ale. Ale was mostly made from barley, but wheat, oats and rye were also used. It may have been the heady fumes from grain fermenting in a spoilt storage pit (see page 28) that gave the Celts the idea of brewing. They also drank mead, which they made from the honey of wild bees.

Yet despite their love of food and drink, the Celts were very figure conscious. According to a Greek writer, any Celtic warrior who put on too much weight and exceeded the "standard length of girdle" was fined.

A farmer's work

Celtic farmers grew wheat and barley as their main crops. They also grew some oats and rye, peas and lentils. Flax was cultivated for its linseed oil which was used as fuel for lamps and for curing animal skins.

Corn was cut with iron sickles. The tough husks were removed by drying them in an oven, or by setting fire to a handful of ears at a time, and beating out the grains with a stick as the husks burnt off. The grain for breadmaking was stored in pots in the granaries, while seed corn was buried in storage pits. These pits were closed with a wooden or stone lid, sealed with clay, and were not opened until it was time for sowing.

Looking after the domestic animals was an important part of the farmer's job. In winter sheep grazed on stubble, but cattle had to be stalled and fed with hay and also bark, which was stripped off in the spring and dried. Elm and lime leaves were stored in pits for winter feed. In summer, sheep and cattle were driven to moors and mountain pastures by herders, who stayed with them until the end of the season.

Attempts are now being made at Butser in Hampshire to reconstruct an Iron Age farm. Archaeologists are using primitive tools and farming methods to grow the type of crops known to the Celts, and to breed similar animals to theirs. In this way they hope to find out more about the Celtic farmer's way of life and his crop yield.

▲ Milk and wool were obtained from the small brown Soay sheep. Cattle were kept for their meat and milk, and also for ploughing, while pigs were kept wherever there were forests with beechmast and acorns for them to feed on.

▼ The woad plant was grown by the Celts for its blue dye. The leaves were crushed and boiled, and the blue liquid was used to dye cloth, and sometimes to paint the face and body.

▲ A farmer ploughing his field. It was very hard work guiding the plough.

► The Celts invented the balanced sickle, bending backwards from the handle (right). It is still used today in some parts of the world for harvesting.

The plough on the left was found in a bog. It has a hard wooden ploughshare. Some ploughs had iron shares.

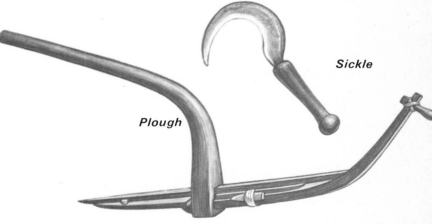

Sickle

Plough

► Celtic fields seen from the air. Their low banks, or "lynchets", cast shadows that show up better from the air than from the ground. The fields were fairly small. Most of them could be ploughed by a man in a 6-8 hour day.

Celtic fields can still be seen on some hillsides, but sadly they are being ploughed away by modern farmers.

The bronzesmith

▲ A bronze shield-boss found at Wandsworth in London. To make this hollow shield-boss, a smith hammered a lump of bronze into the shape of a cup. The flowing design of birds' heads was then slowly cut into the metal with a sharp iron tool.

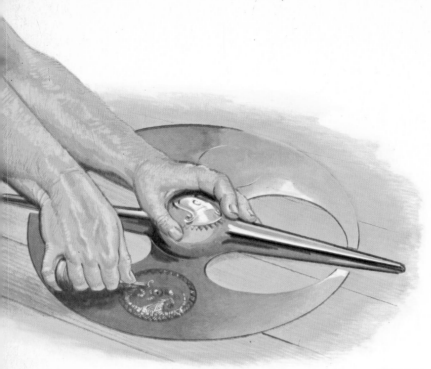

◄ A bronzesmith engraving a pattern on the centrepiece of a shield. The pattern was cut with a graver, a tool with an edge like a screwdriver. The smith rocked it from side to side by turning his wrist, marking the metal with a zigzag line.

▲ In 1971 picnickers found a hoard of Celtic bronzes hidden among rocks on a mountain in Wales. This curved sheet was the centre of a long wooden shield. In the middle is a spiral with three arms, the "triskele" pattern that Celtic artists often drew.

The Celtic bronzesmith was a skilled craftsman, and his work was highly prized by the chiefs and warriors. He fashioned bronze hilts and scabbards for their iron swords, and made fine shields and helmets and chariot fittings.

Bronze is mainly copper mixed with a small amount of tin. It is a shiny, golden metal. Copper and tin are found in fewer places than iron, so bronze objects were more expensive than iron ones. In Celtic times copper ore was found in the mountains of Ireland, Wales, Scotland, Germany, Austria and south-east Europe. The ore was melted down and pure copper extracted. Tin was rarer, but was mined in Cornwall, Brittany, Spain and Germany. Traders brought ingots of copper and tin to trade with the bronzesmiths.

In their workshops the smiths cast the copper and tin into thin bronze sheets, each containing different amounts of tin. Softer bronze, with less tin, could be used for many purposes, but where strength was important, as in the rivets to hold pieces of metal together, bronze with more tin was used. The smith could tell by the brittleness of the sheets which one to use. He shaped objects by casting or hammering, and decorated them by engraving with hard iron tools. Because iron rusts away, very few of these tools have been found.

Casting

To cast small bronze objects, the smith had to make a clay mould. First he carved an exact model in beeswax and coated this with clay, leaving a hole at one end. When the clay was dry, the smith heated it. The wax melted and ran out of the hole, leaving a cavity inside the mould. The smith then poured molten bronze from a crucible into the mould. When it cooled he broke open the mould and the object was ready.

▼ An exquisitely fashioned boar cast in bronze.

▶ This graceful figure of a dancer was also made by casting.

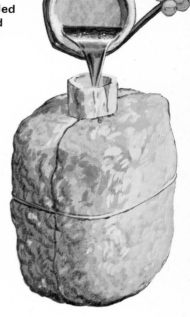

Repoussé

Many Celtic ornaments are decorated with designs that stand out in relief. This was done by hammering the designs out from the back, a method of metalworking called "repoussé".

The cap for a chariot pony, shown on the right, is a fine example of Celtic artistry. The smith beat the bronze into shape, then placed it upside-down on a soft surface to hammer out the curving patterns.

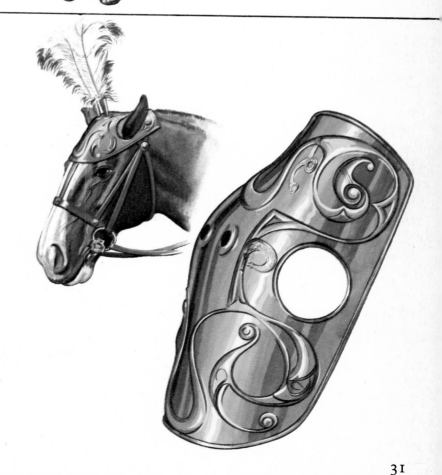

▲ This beautifully decorated silver cauldron was found at Gundestrup in Denmark, although it was probably made somewhere in central Europe. It measures 42 cm high and 69 cm across. The mysterious figures of gods and goddesses were once covered with thin gold foil, and their eyes filled in with red and blue glass.

Torcs

Gold torcs were worn around the neck with the decorated loop terminals at the front. This torc was made of a mixture of silver and gold. The eight twisted strands were each formed of eight twisted wires. The torc was flexible, and the ends could be gently pulled apart to put it on.

Work in precious metals

The Celts loved the gleam of gold and the glitter of silver. Warriors expected kings to reward them for their valour with gifts of torcs, armlets and rings. As a result the goldsmith's work was much in demand.

Goldsmiths worked in hot, smoky workshops. They mixed gold and silver in clay crucibles over a charcoal fire, using bellows to make the fire hotter. Their tools were of bone and iron. When making a torc, the goldsmith used a chisel to cut two round discs into long spiral strands. After shaping, these were twisted together and the terminals were fixed on to the ends.

The Celts were also experts at working with silver. At least three smiths worked on the Gundestrup cauldron shown opposite. The figures were hammered out from the back by the repoussé method described on page 31. Then the sheets were turned over and the animals' coats were filled in with a curved punch. A round punch was used for the leopard's spots, and for belts. To make different scenes on the inside and outside, the sheets were decorated separately and soldered together back to back. An iron rim held them together. They were then fastened to the bowl which had been beaten into shape from a sheet of silver.

▲ The Celts began to mint coins of gold and silver in the late 3rd century BC. The designs were copied from Greek and Roman coins, especially from a coin that on one side had the head of the god Apollo, and on the other his chariot and horses. Gradually these became distorted on the Celtic coins until they were scarcely recognizable.

Each torc had two terminals, which were soldered over the ends of the twisted strands. The terminals were hollow; one Celtic craftsman hid a small gold coin inside a terminal he had made, perhaps for luck. A terminal was made by "waste wax" casting (see page 31). The curved ridges were carved on the wax model. The other decoration was engraved on the surface after the clay mould was broken open. To make a contrast of light and shade, the craftsman hammered criss-cross lines between some of the curved ridges.

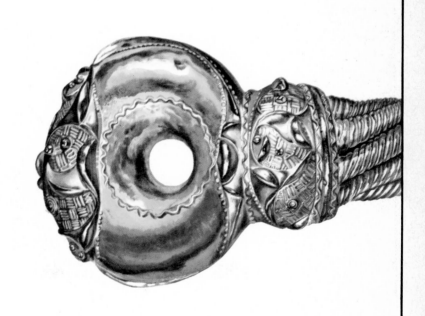

Making a chariot

Celtic chariots were made of wood, but gleamed with bronze and iron fittings and ornaments. The framework had to be as light as possible; the ponies used by the Celts were small and had to pull the chariot and its two occupants, often over rough ground.

To make a chariot, a carpenter joined boards together for the floor. He used joints and wooden pins, not metal nails. Beneath the floor he fixed the axle for the wheels, and a long pole to connect the body of the chariot to the ponies. They were harnessed to it by a yoke. Wicker screens formed the sides, but the front and back were open. When the carpenter had finished the framework, the wheels were made by a skilled wheelwright and iron tyres were put on by a blacksmith.

To drive the chariot, the charioteer climbed in from the back, along with his passenger. He held the reins, and made the ponies go faster by using a whip or a goad.

▲ A drawing of a chariot taken from a Celtic gold coin. Chariots were shown on coins until about 90 BC, when they stopped being used in battle in France. Chariots continued to be used in Britain until well into the Christian era.

▼ The yoke for the ponies was carved from oak, and was lighter than the yokes for oxen. The reins passed through bronze rings called "terrets" to bits in the ponies' mouths.

▼ Some tools used in chariot-making. Iron tools like these have been found complete with their wooden handles at Glastonbury in Somerset. The carpenter used the saw to cut up wood. He made planks with the adze and trimmed them with the chisel. The wooden mallet was used to hammer jointed pieces of wood together.

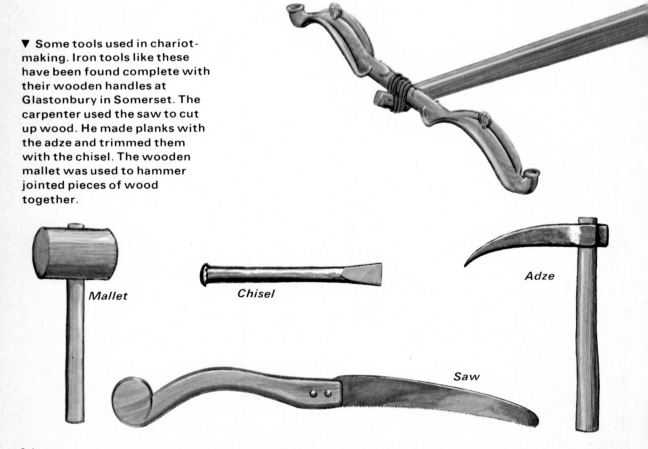

Mallet

Chisel

Adze

Saw

The Celts used chariots for travelling and for driving to battle. They did not fight in chariots. Before a battle, warriors would drive up and down in front of the enemy, boasting and shouting insults. Then they were set down and fought on foot, while the charioteer waited nearby. After the battle the warrior would jump into his chariot, either to chase the fleeing enemy or to make his own escape.

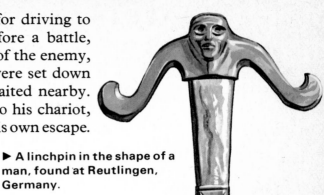

▶ A linchpin in the shape of a man, found at Reutlingen, Germany.

▲ The craftsman is hammering a linchpin into the end of the axle to keep the wheel on. The iron tyre was heated and fitted over the rim of the wheel while it was still red-hot. As the tyre cooled it shrank to fit tightly onto the wheel.

◀ A chariot wheel with an iron tyre found on the muddy shore of the River Tyne at Ryton in Durham. The massive hub was 40 cm long. The outer end of each spoke fitted into a hole in the rim which was made from a single piece of wood. The wheel measured 98 cm across.

35

The blacksmith

The blacksmith was a very useful member of the community. Most of the things he made were for everyday use, not for display. He made iron collars for people who could not afford gold torcs, tools for other craftsmen, slave-chains, and tyres for the chariots.

The Celts could get iron ore easily. It did not have to be mined like copper. The ore was near the surface of the ground and could be dug from shallow pits.

It was the Greeks who taught the Celts how to work iron. Smelting the iron from its ore was not difficult. But the "bloom" of iron that formed at the bottom of the furnace was just a soft, spongy mass. It was no use until it had been heated red-hot in a charcoal fire, and hammered on an anvil. This made it hard enough to use for tools.

The Celtic blacksmith could not cast iron in the way that the bronzesmith cast bronze. He could not heat his furnace to a high enough temperature. Instead he had to shape iron objects by "forging". This meant heating up the metal in the fire and hammering it into shape while it was still soft and malleable. Blacksmiths needed a lot of charcoal for their furnaces. Many trees had to be cut down to keep their fires burning, and large areas of forest probably disappeared as a result.

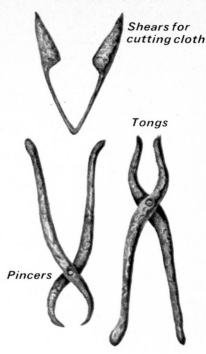

Shears for cutting cloth

Tongs

Pincers

▲ Some iron tools made by a blacksmith.

▼ Smelting iron ore. Layers of charcoal and iron ore were put into a furnace built of clay over a shallow clay-lined pit. Skin bellows with a clay nozzle were used to pump air into the furnace to make it hotter. When the temperature reached 800-900°C, a "bloom" of iron formed in the pit.

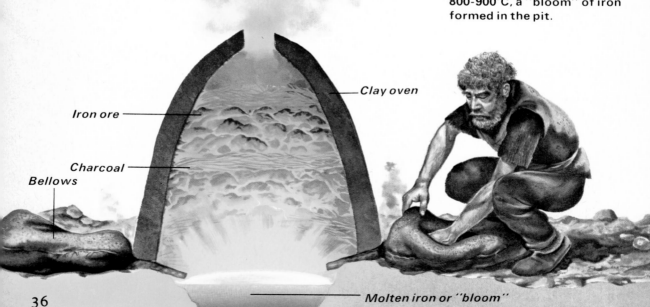

Iron ore

Clay oven

Charcoal

Bellows

Molten iron or "bloom"

► Some of the blacksmith's work was decorative as well as useful. These fine "firedogs" with their graceful deer heads were forged with tongs and hammer. We do not know exactly how they were used. Logs may have been laid across them as in the picture, so that a draught could get underneath to make them burn. Another theory is that the logs were propped upright against the firedogs.

▼ Captives were imprisoned in slave-chains, which had five or six neck-rings. A ring was put round the captive's neck, and fastened by passing the whole of the rest of the chain through the loop. The chain was made of iron rings that were pinched together in the middle, like a figure 8. People believed that this form of link was only invented in the 18th century AD, to make ships' chains stronger, until the remains of Celtic slave-chains were found.

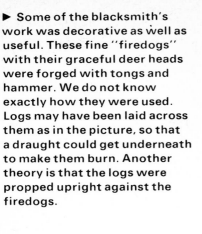

The Celtic year

The main purpose of Celtic festivals was to ensure a good harvest, so they took place at times of the year that were important for farmers. People gathered together from outlying farms at the tribe's holy place, possibly inside a hillfort, and there was much feasting and merry-making. Above all, however, the festivals were religious occasions, and sacrifices were made to the gods to encourage fertility.

IMBOLC (1st February)
This festival took place at lambing time and was to celebrate the fact that the ewes were producing milk. In the picture girls are milking ewes and offering the milk to a wooden statue of the goddess Brigid under a sacred oak tree. Brigid was associated with the oak and with fire.

BELTAINE (1st May)
The name of this festival means "Bel's fire" or "goodly fire". It may have been a festival of the god Belenos. At Beltaine the Celts lit bonfires topped by poles symbolizing the sacred oak tree. Then druids drove cattle through the flames to purify them and protect them from disease. The druids also made sacrifices and prayed to the gods for a fruitful year. Beltaine fires were still lit in Scotland in quite recent times.

LUGHNASA (1st August)
"Lughnasa" or "the feast of Lug" was a harvest festival connected with a god called Lug in Ireland, Lleu in Wales and Lugus in France. At this festival people put on a play which the rest of the tribe watched. The young warrior in the foreground represents Lug. He has built a granary and is now fighting a "giant" (really just a tall member of the tribe) to get food for his men.

SAMAIN (1st November)
Samain, "the end of summer", was the most important festival of all. It was the beginning of the new year. To make the land prosper, the Celts celebrated the marriage of the tribal god to a nature goddess. The eve of Samain was believed to be a magic time with many strange events such as the one illustrated. Girls who had been changed into swans regained their human shape and could join their human lovers.

The druids

The druids were the Celts' priests. The name "druid" may mean "knowledge of the oak"; the Celts believed that the oak tree was sacred.

The most important function of the druids was to perform religious ceremonies. They chanted spells and prayers and offered sacrifices to the gods, which probably included human as well as animal victims. The druids were also the tribe's wise men; they handed down the tribal laws and knowledge to later generations. Only boys of royal or noble birth could become druids. The training took many years, as a druid's knowledge had to be learned by heart. Nothing was written down, and all the knowledge was passed on by word of mouth.

▼ A tribe is celebrating its victory over an enemy. Captives are being stripped of their gold torcs and their swords. Druids are hurling these into the lake, to give thanks to the water goddess who has given them victory in battle.

Remains of a wooden platform like this one have been found at La Tène, on the shores of Lake Neuchâtel, in Switzerland.

Some of the druids lived with chiefs in the hillforts, others lived in sanctuaries in forests. Ceremonies were held at these sanctuaries. After a victory in battle, torcs and weapons were taken from the defeated warriors and offered up to the gods. Some druids left great piles of captured treasure in the forest clearings.

Shrines were also built in hillforts and at the source of rivers. Some contained human heads or carvings of them. The shrine at Roquepertuse in France was entered through a brightly-painted stone archway, with human skulls placed in niches in the upright pillars.

After the Romans had conquered France and Britain, they hunted down the druids, perhaps because they had led the resistance to the Roman armies. Many druids were put to death. Others changed sides, and became priests in the new Roman temples. Gradually all the ancient knowledge of the Celtic druids was lost.

▲ This wise face, with its strange crown, may be a portrait of a famous druid. It is part of the handle of a wine flagon found in a royal grave in Germany.

Religion and beliefs

Gods and goddesses

The Celts worshipped many gods and goddesses. Caesar wrote that the whole people "is much given to religion". But because the Celts did not write about their beliefs, there are many aspects that we do not understand.

Roman authors give some information, but it is hard to believe that the Celts would have revealed many secrets of their religion to their enemies. The names of some Celtic gods are known because in Roman times altars were dedicated to them and to the Roman god they were thought to be most like. The Celts themselves made statues of their gods and goddesses, but did not always inscribe them with their names. Deities are also described in stories told in Ireland and written down in Christian times, but these were written down long after their worship had officially ceased.

It seems that, just as the Celts were never one united people, so their gods were not regarded as a single divine family

like the Greek and Roman gods. Each tribe worshipped its own gods. However there were basic "types" of gods. Many tribes worshipped a young warrior god. There were also horned gods who were shown either with stags' antlers or with rams' or bulls' horns. Some gods were famous for their healing powers.

In statues and in stories, the deities are usually shown with a human shape; they are often beautiful and splendidly dressed. Many were kind to humans and helped them. Sometimes a god fell in love with a mortal woman; famous warriors were often said to have been fathered by a god. On the other hand, the dreaded Morrigan was a war goddess who appeared in hideous form to haunt doomed warriors.

The gods and goddesses inhabited the Otherworld, a place where life went on much as in the real world. The Celts believed that after death they joined the gods in the Otherworld. For them death was the "centre of a long life", not the end.

◄ An unknown god and goddess on the silver sheets forming the great cauldron found at Gundestrup in Denmark. They are both wearing torcs and are shown much larger than their attendants, which suggests they are divine.

► The Mothers, a stone carving of three mother goddesses, holding the fruits of the earth in their laps. The Celts thought that three was a magic number, and there were many triple gods and goddesses.

► The head of a bronze statue of a god found at Bouray in France. The god was squatting with his very short legs crossed. Around his neck is a torc. His menacing eyes were made of inlaid glass.

Sacred animals

The Celts worshipped animals as well as gods and goddesses. The boar was revered for its fierceness and courage. One story described a giant boar that rampaged over Wales and Cornwall with a comb and scissors between its ears. There were also sacred hounds, bulls and other animals.

Birds could be either good or evil. Three cranes of the god Midir were believed to take away a warrior's courage, and to discourage guests from staying at his house. Ravens made the Celts think of battlefields and death, but the birds of the goddess Rhiannon sang so beautifully to feasting heroes that they forgot the time, and years passed away as they listened.

The cult of the severed head

The Celts considered that the severed heads of their enemies were sacred. They cut them off and displayed them on posts around their homes, or embalmed them in cedar oil and kept them in special boxes. Some were displayed in shrines.

Storytelling

The Celts loved to listen to stories at feasts and festivals. There were many Celtic stories, and the most popular were about the exploits of heroes.

Many Irish tales told about King Conchobar of Ulster and his warriors, in particular Cu Chulainn who performed incredible feats of valour. In one story, "The Cattle Raid of Cooley", Cu Chulainn defended the whole of Ulster single-handed against an army from Connaught sent to steal the magic Brown Bull of Cooley.

Stories like these were told by bards, who knew them off by heart. They also composed poems in praise of their chief, some more than 40 verses long. Bards were rewarded with gold. If they thought their pay was not generous enough, they would compose a "satire" to make the chief look foolish, like this one:

"He has no wealth
   Nothing in the way of beauty
   Nothing but feeble wit
   Good for nothing but empty talk."

A more learned storyteller and poet was called a "fili". The fili trained for 12 years, learning by heart not only stories and poems but the history of the tribe.

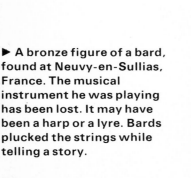

▶ A bronze figure of a bard, found at Neuvy-en-Sullias, France. The musical instrument he was playing has been lost. It may have been a harp or a lyre. Bards plucked the strings while telling a story.

THE STORY OF BRICRIU'S FEAST

1. Bricriu was a lord of Ulster. He wished to stir up rivalry between the three heroes of Ulster, Cu Chulainn, Loeghaire and Conall. He built a new house and invited them to a feast.

4. The heroes were next sent to fight magic monsters. Only Cu Chulainn did not run away. But the others still refused him the Portion.

2. Bricriu spoke to each hero in turn, promising them all the Champion's Portion. He hoped they would fight over it.

3. Then Bricriu said that the winner would be the one whose wife first entered the house. The wives ran to the house. Cu Chulainn lifted up the wall to let his wife in first. The men nearly came to blows.

5. Then a huge giant appeared. His axe had "an edge that would cut a hair aloft in the wind". He challenged the heroes to cut off his head and to let him cut off theirs the next night. Loeghaire and Conall were afraid.

6. But Cu Chulainn jumped up and cut off the giant's head. Next night he lay down with his head on the block. The giant brought down only the back of the axe against his neck, praising him as the bravest warrior of all.

A fight to the death

For the Celts fighting was an art. Boys were trained from an early age in the use of different weapons, and taught how to defend themselves with a long shield. They also learned to use words as weapons, and never to show fear.

An attack by one tribe on another usually began with a warrior challenging one of the other side to single combat. Despite their warlike natures, the Celts believed in fair play, and there were strict unwritten laws about combat. A warrior could be attacked by only one man at a time. Before fighting, each warrior would try to destroy the other's confidence. One might drive noisily up and down in his chariot, performing balancing tricks with his glittering weapons, to show his superior skill. Then they would shout abuse at each other: "I have come, a wild boar of the herd . . . to thrust you beneath the waters of the pool. Here is one who will crush you. It is I who will slay you, for it is I who can."

A Celtic warrior was bound by honour at all times. He might be forced to fight a good friend or even his foster brother if they followed different chiefs. A warrior's loyalty was always to his chief.

A Celt was not afraid of death. Above all else he wished to be known as a great fighter and fearless hero, whose exploits would live on after his death in the stories told by bards. Given a choice between a short and glorious life and a long one ending in sleepy old age, no warrior would hesitate in choosing death and glory.

Helmet

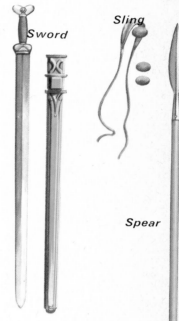

Sword

Sling

Spear

Shield

▼ This Roman statue shows a naked Celtic warrior dying in battle, with his wooden shield. Some Celts went into battle wearing only a torc around their necks.

▶ Some fine examples of Celtic weapons and armour. The beautifully decorated bronze helmet and shield were probably never used in battle but were for rituals only.

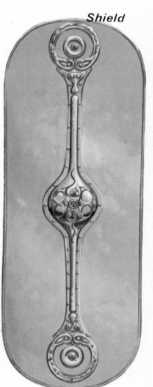

Burial and the Otherworld

The Celts believed in life after death. The dead were buried with their possessions so that they would be prepared for the journey to the Otherworld. This is why Celtic graves have proved such a rich store for the archaeologist.

Chiefs were buried with food and wine, weapons and clothing, and rich jewellery. Many royal graves were marked with a great mound of earth, called a barrow or tumulus. In northern France and in Yorkshire, chiefs have been found buried in their chariots, along with the harness of their chariot ponies.

Warriors were buried with their weapons. Other men were given a few pots of food and drink and were buried in their clothes, sometimes with their ornaments. Women were often buried dressed with their bead necklaces and other jewellery, and with pots of food and drink. But some bodies, probably those of servants or criminals, were disposed of very casually, with no grave at all. They were simply thrown into old rubbish pits, and covered with earth.

▶ The burial of a warrior. His sword is at his side and his wooden shield is being placed over his head and body. The warrior's spear has been broken into two pieces as a symbol of his death. No food or drink has been provided for his spirit.

▼ The burial grave of a chief. The chief's body has been burnt on a funeral pyre and the ashes placed in the wooden box on the burial couch. Three large amphorae of wine and several joints of meat including a whole pig are buried with the ashes to provide refreshment for the chief's spirit.

Famous Celts

Bellovesus (4th century BC) was a nephew of Ambicatus, chief of the Bituriges tribe from southern Germany. He was appointed to lead a large group of Celts, from a number of different tribes, who wanted to find new lands. Bellovesus took 200,000 men and their families in safety across the Alps into Italy. Some travelled on foot, driving pack-horses, others were in chariots or wagons. They settled in the rich lands of the River Po, waging war on the Etruscans.

Vercingetorix (1st century BC) was an Arvernian chief from central France. His father had been put to death by other chiefs for becoming too powerful. Vercingetorix was a born leader and a brilliant commander. He raised a huge army against Caesar in 52 BC which would have succeeded in driving the Romans out of France (known then as Gaul) if all the tribes had united under him. However his orders were disobeyed and some of the tribes held back from joining him until too late. After many fierce battles and a long siege at Alesia, Vercingetorix gave himself up. Caesar kept him in prison in Rome for six years and then put him to death.

▲ A coin bearing the head of Vercingetorix.

Ambiorix (1st century BC) and the elderly Catuvolcus were joint chiefs of the Eburones, whose lands were in the Low Countries. When Caesar waged war on the Celts in France, Ambiorix fought against him. In 54 BC the Eburones massacred a Roman force, and then joined a league of Celts and Germans. This formidable alliance did not drive Caesar out of France, because the Aedui, although they were Celts, fought on the Roman side. Caesar ravaged the lands of his enemies one by one. Ambiorix managed to escape capture and remained on the run until his death.

▲ A statue of Ambiorix.

Cassivellaunus (1st century BC) was a powerful chief in southern Britain at the time of Caesar's second raid in 54 BC. When Caesar landed Cassivellaunus was fighting another tribe, the Trinovantes. Eventually however he took over the campaign against the Romans. Caesar laid waste to Cassivellaunus's lands but could not find his hillfort until the way to it was betrayed by the Trinovantes. Caesar fell upon the fort and captured many men. After a desperate struggle, Cassivellaunus surrendered to Caesar.

Diviciacus (1st century BC) was chief of the Aedui, from east-central France. When tribes from across the River Rhine threatened to attack his people in 61 BC, Diviciacus travelled to Rome to ask the Senate for military aid. This was refused but Diviciacus remained friendly to the Romans, and helped Julius Caesar in his conquest of Gaul. However his younger brother, Dumnorix, who led an anti-Roman faction in the tribe, took his place as chief by intrigue. Diviciacus was trained as a druid, and it may have been from him that Caesar obtained the information about Celtic religion described in his book about the conquest of Gaul.

Cartimandua (1st century AD) was queen of the Brigantes, a tribe with lands extending over much of the north of England. She was friendly towards the Romans. Her husband, Venutius, however, hated the Romans, and the tribe was divided into two factions. When Caratacus fled to her for protection, Cartimandua handed him over to the Romans. She quarrelled with her husband and married his shield-bearer, Vellocatus. When she tried to make him king, civil war broke out. Cartimandua was rescued by a Roman army and went into exile.

Caratacus (1st century AD) was one of the sons of Cunobelin, king of the Catuvellauni. Their lands stretched from Kent to the Cotswolds. With his brother Togodumnus, he led a great army to try to stop the Roman army crossing the River Medway, Kent, in AD 43. When the Celts were defeated, Caratacus fled to south Wales. He led Welsh tribes against the Romans, using guerilla tactics. When at last he was forced to fight a pitched battle, he was defeated. He sought refuge at the court of Cartimandua, queen of the Brigantes, but she handed him over to the Romans in AD 51. He ended his days in captivity in Rome.

▲ Boudicca riding in her chariot.

Boudicca (1st century AD), often referred to as Boadicea, was a queen of the Iceni, a tribe in Norfolk. A Roman writer wrote about her: "She was huge of frame, terrifying of aspect, and with a harsh voice. A great mass of bright red hair fell to her knees . . ." After the death of her husband Prasutagus in AD 61, Boudicca was not recognized as queen by the Romans, who treated her and her daughters very harshly. The tribe rose in revolt and plundered the Roman towns of Camulodunum (Colchester), Verulamium (St Albans) and Londinium (London). At last a Roman general defeated Boudicca's army in a set battle, when 80,000 of her followers died. Boudicca poisoned herself.

What became of the Celts?

Between about 500 and 250 BC, the Celts were the most powerful people north of the Alps. They stretched across Europe from Spain in the west to Russia in the east; from the Baltic Sea in the north to the Adriatic in the south.

But during this time the Romans too were becoming powerful in central Italy. In the 3rd century BC they defeated the Celts who had settled in northern Italy. The Roman Empire grew gradually larger and larger. By the end of the 1st century AD all the Celtic areas of Europe, apart from Ireland and much of Scotland, had become part of the Roman Empire.

▲ Compare the flowing design of the Celtic motif on the left with the detail on the right taken from the Book of Kells, an Irish manuscript dating from the 9th century AD.

▲ This carved stone head decorated a Roman temple, but was the work of a Celtic craftsman.

The Romans defeated the Celts because their warriors were disciplined and better organized. In other ways the Celts were if anything superior to the Romans: in their use of metals, for example, and their decorative techniques.

In each conquered area, Celtic tribes were forced to leave their hillforts, and the defences were pulled down. The Romans made fine straight roads, running across country, and built new towns at important junctions and river crossings. Celtic life went on in the new towns, under pro-Roman chiefs, but the craftsmen found themselves out of work. Their hand-made ornaments were not wanted as mass-produced ones from Roman workshops were cheaper. Fighting between tribes was stopped by the Romans, with the result that no-one wanted to buy their weapons and shields.

When France, or Gaul as it was then called, was conquered in the 1st century BC, Gallic craftsmen sailed to Britain, where their work was still in demand.

In AD 43 the Romans invaded Britain. The Celts called Belgae, who lived in south-east England, resisted bitterly, but other tribes, who had been attacked by the Belgae, fought on the side of the Romans. It was not long before the Celts of south-east England were defeated and left their hillforts for lowland towns. Craftsmen fled to the north and west.

In Wales and the north of England, the Romans did not fully conquer the Celts but subdued them by building strong

▲ A Celtic bronze plate decorated with the traditional "triskele" pattern.

▲ The pattern lives on in the "three legs of man", the symbol of the Isle of Man.

forts linked by good roads. Walls were built from the east to the west coast across northern England and the Lowlands of Scotland, to mark the frontier against the wild Picts. The Picts and the Celts in Ireland never came under Roman rule.

After nearly 400 years, the Roman armies left Britain to defend Rome against barbarian attacks. The Romano-Britons, the Celtic people of Roman Britain, had to defend themselves against the Picts in Scotland and marauding Saxons from the Low Countries. Strong Celtic kingdoms arose in Wales and in the north.

▲ A stone cross erected by Christians in the 10th century AD. The decoration is unmistakably Celtic in origin.

From about AD 450 Angles, Saxons and Jutes left northern Europe to settle in England. Through inter-marriage, the Celts became mixed with them and, later, with Viking settlers from Scandinavia.

The Anglo-Saxons were heathen, but the Romano-Britons had become Christian. In AD 432, St Patrick began to convert the Irish Celts. Later St Columba converted the Picts in Scotland. Christian monks introduced writing, and made beautifully illustrated copies of the Gospels. Many of the designs they used were derived from the old Celtic art. Celtic tendrils and curling patterns were also used to decorate the stone crosses put up in many places.

In Ireland, the Celtic way of life, with fighting and feasting, had continued without interruption. The ancient stories about gods and heroes were still being told. Some of these stories were written down by the monks, and have been preserved into modern times.

Celtic languages are still spoken in the British Isles and in Brittany, in the form of Scottish and Irish Gaelic, Welsh and Breton. Although these languages developed in different ways over the centuries, they all have their roots in the language spoken by the ancient Celts.

The story of the Celts

1000-400 BC

At the beginning of this period the ancestors of the Celts were living in central Europe; by the end they had spread to western Europe and perhaps also to Britain. They were warlike people, and lived in defended settlements. Their bronzesmiths were very skilled at making swords and armour. After about 700 BC they began to use iron. Iron weapons were more efficient than bronze ones so their use became widespread. Some of these early Celts were farmers; others were miners, working in salt mines and copper mines in the Alps.

400-300 BC

During this period many Celts living in central Europe set out to find new lands. About 200,000 Celts left their homeland to cross the Alps. The women and children travelled in wagons. The Celts began to settle in the rich lands of northern Italy, where they fought the Etruscans who lived there, and succeeded in destroying many Etruscan cities. Their raids took them as far south as Sicily, and they even sacked Rome.

▲ The Celts cross the Alps.

300-280 BC

Many more Celts left central Europe, travelling south-east, to seek new lands and riches. They stormed into Bulgaria and Macedonia (now part of Greece). The famous leader Brennus led an army of 150,000 men on foot, and 20,000 cavalry. Their families went with them in covered wagons. Brennus and his army fought many battles against the inhabitants of the lands they invaded.

280-200 BC

▲ The sack of Delphi.

In 279 BC Brennus and his army fought the Greeks and sacked the famous Greek temple of the god Apollo at Delphi. They carried off the treasures that had been sent to the temple from faraway lands. But the Celts' success came to an end with the death of Brennus. It was said that Apollo wounded Brennus, in revenge for the attack on his temple. Brennus drank too much and killed himself, and the Greeks drove his army out of their country.

After this defeat, the Celts settled where they could. Some founded the city of Belgrade in modern Yugoslavia. Others wandered as far east as the Sea of Azov, in Russia. One band crossed the Dardanelles into Anatolia, the modern eastern Turkey. They ravaged the land, and took tribute from many rich cities, until they were defeated by the ruler of Pergamon. He forced them to settle on poor soil, which was not good for farming, near the modern Turkish capital of Ankara. For a long time afterwards this region was called "Galatia", after the Gauls who had settled there.

▲ A spearman of the Gaesatae.

In northern Italy, the Celts were being threatened by the Romans and their expanding Empire, and they sent for fighting men from across the Alps to help them in their struggle. The famous Gaesatae, or "spear-men", came to their aid. The Gaesatae dedicated their bodies to the gods, and fought naked apart from gold torcs. In 225 BC, at the battle of Telamon, the Celtic army was trapped between two Roman forces and destroyed. After this, the Celtic settlements south of the Alps were ruled by the Romans.

200-58 BC

Roman armies began to conquer the Celtic tribes living across the Alps, in France, which they called "Gaul".

58-52 BC

The great Roman soldier Julius Caesar continued the conquest of Gaul. He wrote his memoirs of the war, which describe the Celts and how they lived and fought. Caesar also made two raids on south-east Britain, in 55 and 54 BC.

In Gaul, Vercingetorix, the last leader of the free Gauls, was captured by Caesar after a long siege of the hillfort of Alesia, in 52 BC. The Gauls were finally conquered, and began to adopt Roman ways.

AD43

In AD 43, in the reign of the Emperor Claudius, another Roman army landed in Britain. After bitter resistance, the south and east of the country were conquered. Hillforts were besieged and captured. The inhabitants were driven out to build new towns in the valleys, under pro-Roman rulers. They began to live like Romans. But in the north and west, and in Ireland, the Celtic way of life went on.

▲ Celts are forced to leave their hillfort.

The Celtic world

From 1200 BC, the Celtic tribes north of the Alps began to send out colonies into new territories and spread their influence over a large area, as you can see from the map. Some 900 years later the Romans of central Italy began also to expand over vast tracts of territory. The Celts were gradually beaten back and conquered by the disciplined Roman legions. Except in Ireland, they were brought one by one into the Roman Empire and slowly lost their identity.

But although the Celts were overrun and absorbed into the Roman Empire, it is still possible today, 2,000 years later, to find traces of their existence. In most countries of Celtic settlement there are remains of hillforts and Celtic shrines, overgrown but still recognizable. Some of these are marked on the map. Archaeologists have uncovered a great many Celtic artefacts—jewellery, weapons, tools; and many more still remain to be discovered. And traces of the Celtic language survive in numerous place names as well as more directly in the Celtic languages spoken today: Scottish and Irish Gaelic, Welsh and Breton. Although they left no written records, the Celts have not been forgotten.

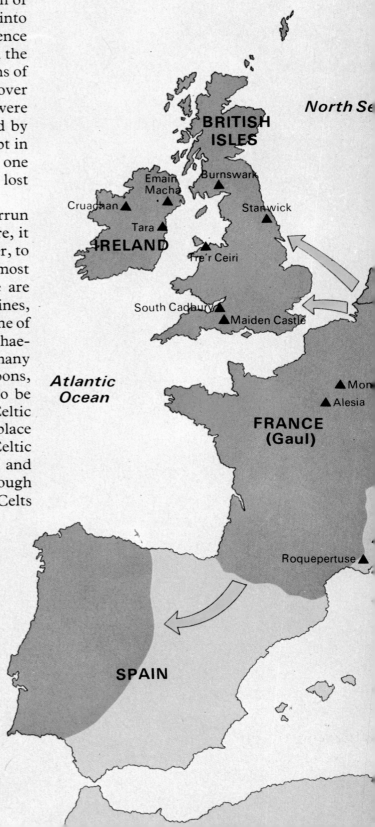

- ▆ Area occupied by Celtic peoples

- ▢ Area occupied by other peoples

- ▲ Celtic sites

The map gives some idea of the very large areas occupied by Celtic tribes in the last centuries before Christ. Celtic languages were spoken from Portugal in the west to Anatolia (eastern Turkey) in the east. Some of the Celtic place-names and river-names were adopted by other peoples who conquered the Celts in later times. The Teutons, in Germany, for example, kept the Celtic names for the rivers Elbe and Weser, and in England the Anglo-Saxons used many Celtic names (including "Ouse", which means "water"). So even in areas where the people today are not of Celtic origin, local Celtic names remind us that the Celts once lived there.

The arrows on the map indicate the direction in which Celtic tribes moved in their migrations. These have been traced by the evidence of archaeology and from the writings of Greek and Roman authors.

The map also shows some of the sites of famous Celtic hillforts and shrines.

Baltic Sea

Slavs

Germans

River Rhine

● Waldalgesheim

is

euneburg ▲

▲ Manching

River Danube

Scythians

RUSSIA

▲ La Tène

▲ Hallstatt

● Strettweg

Black Sea

River Po

Etruscans

emont

ilia

Adriatic Sea

Thracians

TURKEY

Telamon ●

Rome ●

ITALY

GREECE

Aegean Sea

● Pergamon

Delphi ●

diterranean Sea

World history 500 BC to AD 300

Celts	Europe	Asia
500 BC		
The Hallstatt Celts were using iron. Greek writers mention "Keltoi" as living in France and at the source of the River Danube. The beginning of beautiful La Tène art on weapons and shields (500 BC). The Celts invade Italy and sack Rome (400 BC).	The Etruscans are a great civilization in northern Italy. The Persians fail to add Europe to their Empire, and are defeated by the Greeks on land and sea. Civil war (431-404 BC) destroys the Athenian Empire in Greece, and Greece becomes dominated by Alexander the Great of Macedon (336-323 BC).	The time of Confucius in China and Gautama Buddha in India. The Chinese use cast iron for tools and bronze for weapons. The use of iron spreads to India from the west. After Alexander the Great's conquests in India, an Empire is set up. Buddhism becomes established over most of India.
300 BC		
Tribes from northern France settle in Yorkshire. Celts invading south-east Europe attack Delphi in Greece (279 BC) and cross into Anatolia. They are defeated in 240 BC at Pergamon. The Celts in Italy are defeated by the Romans at Telamon (225 BC).	The Romans dominate Italy by defeating neighbouring tribes. By 146 BC they control the Mediterranean Sea. Tribes from Denmark invade France, and are defeated by the Romans (120 BC). In 102 BC Goths from Sweden settle near the Black Sea.	China is united by the Emperor Shih Huang Ti, of the Ch'in dynasty (221 BC). He builds the Great Wall, which is 2200 km long. In 200 BC, the Chinese invent the crossbow, the last important weapon to be discovered before firearms. They use acupuncture in medicine.
100 BC		
The development of large hilltop towns in Celtic Europe. Belgic tribes from the Low Countries settle in south-east England. Julius Caesar fights the Celts in France and Britain, and defeats Vercingetorix (52 BC). The Romans invade Britain (AD 43) and defeat Boudicca's rebellion (AD 61).	Roman rule extends to the Rhine and the Danube, and includes Crete and Syria. The republic becomes an Empire under Augustus in 31 BC. Under Nero (AD 54-68) Rome burns down, and many Christians are persecuted.	The Chinese invent a form of horse-collar over 800 years before the modern form is used in Europe. The Han Dynasty (202 BC-AD 220) centres on the River Yangtze. Silk is traded overland and also by sea routes from China to the Roman Empire.
AD 100		
The Romans abandon the conquest of Scotland, and build walls across north Britain. Many foreign cults, and Christianity, take root in Britain and other parts of the Roman Empire. The Celts in the Empire adopt Roman ways and fight in the Roman armies.	The Roman Empire is under attack from barbarians. There are also civil wars caused by men fighting to become Emperor. In AD 251 the Emperor Decius is killed fighting the Goths in the Balkans. In these troubled times, Christianity is spreading.	Yayoi farmers with an advanced form of rice cultivation reach Tohuku in Japan (they had first arrived in the country before 200 BC). Hindu merchants trade iron to stone-using peoples in the East Indies. Buddhism reaches China, where the Han Dynasty ends in AD 220.
AD 300		
Barbarians attack the Roman Empire on many fronts. In Britain, the Picts in the north, Saxons in the east, and Scots from Ireland threaten. The Roman army withdraws to defend Rome. The Britons organize their own defences, and Christian kingdoms are set up in northern Britain and in Wales.	The Huns and other barbarians flood into Europe. Visigoths and Vandals sack Rome itself. The Emperor Constantine (AD 306-337) ends the persecution of Christians. France is ruled by Merovingian kings. In AD 486, Clovis, king of the Franks, becomes a Christian.	The first images of Buddha are carved in China. Pilgrims begin to travel to China from India along the Silk route. Roman traders establish a trading post in south Vietnam. By AD 400, there is a wealthy feudal society in Japan. The foundations of later Japanese institutions are laid.

Africa

Near East

America

		500 BC

In most parts, people live by hunting or very simple farming, but the civilization of Egypt enters the Ptolemaic period in 323 BC. Ironworking spreads from Egypt to Meroe, a kingdom in the Sudan, and from there to West Africa; later, with Bantu-speaking peoples, to the south.

Persia is the most powerful state with its great Empire reaching from Egypt to India. Its religion is Zoroastrianism, a cult with a belief in one god and a system of rewards and punishments after death, which influenced Judaism and Christianity. Alexander the Great conquers many Near East lands.

In Mexico, farmers grow maize, beans and squashes. They do not use metals, but make fine pots, without the potter's wheel. They weave cloth, and make jade figurines. They worship the jaguar, and sacrifice men. In Peru, copper, silver and gold are used, but the smiths cannot make bronze.

300 BC

Euclid teaches mathematics at the great centre of scholars at Alexandria, where there is a famous library. Manetho writes a history of Egypt. The Rosetta Stone is set up (196 BC). Meroitic kings rule over Upper and Lower Nubia.

Most of the Old Testament is written down. Some of the Dead Sea scrolls are written. In 198 BC, Jerusalem is captured by the Seleucid kings of Antioch. The Jews, led by Judas Maccabeus, rebel (166 BC).

In Peru, farmers grow cotton. Brightly-coloured embroidered clothes are buried with the dead. The heads of children are bound up to shape the growing skull. Copper, silver and gold are cast in open moulds, and by the "waste wax" method. Objects are also shaped by hammering, welding and soldering.

100 BC

The Sahara is drying into a desert. With Cleopatra's death (30 BC), Egypt becomes a Roman province. There is much Arab influence in the negroid kingdoms of East Africa, which trade with India. Food production comes to Zimbabwe with people from the north.

Palestine becomes part of the Roman Empire (63 BC). Parthian horsemen wipe out a Roman army under Crassus in Iran (53 BC). Herod is made king of Judaea by the Romans (40 BC). Jesus Christ is born in Jordan, and Christianity spreads to Africa, Spain and France.

Everywhere in the Americas, people live by hunting and fishing except in Mexico, Peru and in the south-west of north America. There, simple farming is practised by the "Basket Makers". In Peru and Mexico, farming is much more advanced, and civilizations are developing.

AD 100

Berber peoples from North Africa cross the Sahara and mix with negro tribes. This leads to the rise of the West African Empires. The kingdom of Ghana is founded by Jews from Cyrenaica (AD 200).

The Emperor Trajan creates the Roman province of Arabia (AD 106), incorporating the Nabataean city of Petra in Jordan. In AD 205, Edessa, in north-west Iraq, becomes the first kingdom to adopt Christianity as its state religion.

In the Proto-Classic period of the Maya culture in Mexico, stone temples are built. In Peru, this is the time of the Classic Period of the Mochica, Nasca, and Tiahuanaco cultures. There is no knowledge of wrought or cast ironwork anywhere in the Americas.

AD 300

The site of Zimbabwe is deserted for hundreds of years. In Nubia live the unknown "X-group" people, who bury their dead in richly-furnished tombs. In AD 380, the Roman Emperor Theodosius orders the pagan temples of Egypt to be closed. Many pagan monuments are wrecked by Christian fanatics.

Monasticism becomes widespread, reaching Europe from the Near East. People go on pilgrimages to Jerusalem. Huge tombs and buildings are carved in the rock at Petra. In AD 362 the Emperor Julian the Apostate's plan to restore the Jewish temple at Jerusalem is ended by a fire-damp explosion.

The beginning of the Classic Period of the Maya culture, in Mexico, sees the building of great temples on pyramids, and of observatories. The Maya use their own form of hieroglyphic writing, and work out a very accurate calendar, but they have no knowledge of the wheel, and make little use of metals.

Glossary

adze a chopping tool with the blade mounted at a right-angle to the handle.

amphora a thick clay jar in which wine was traded (plural "amphorae")

archaeologist one who excavates ancient sites to discover how people lived in the past.

bard a storyteller.

barrow a mound of earth over a grave.

bracae Celtic word for "trousers".

carnyx a Celtic war-trumpet.

crucible a small, thick clay pot for melting metals.

cult car a wheeled vehicle used in religious ceremonies.

druid a Celtic priest.

Hallstatt culture iron-using farmers and warriors who lived in central Europe in around 700 BC.

hillfort a tribal settlement on a hill, defended by ramparts and ditches.

hostages prisoners given as security in an agreement, who will be killed if the agreement is broken.

ingot a shaped block of metal for trading.

La Tène culture iron-using Celts with beautiful art-forms, dating from 500 BC.

linchpin a small bar inserted into the end of the axle of a chariot to keep the wheel in place.

lynchets low banks bordering fields.

palisade a wooden fence.

rampart the wall around a hillfort.

ritual religious ceremony.

shrine a building for worship.

sickle a tool for harvesting grain.

storage pit a hole in the ground with a sealed lid for storing grain.

terminal the decorated end of a torc.

torc a neck-ring of twisted strands.

triskele a pattern with three lines coming from the centre.

Urnfield culture bronze-using warriors and farmers, ancestors of the Celts, living about 1200 BC in central Europe.

wattle and daub a wall of frames plastered with clay on both sides.

Index